Milo Writes

MILO WRITES

poems by
Milo Wright

A.K.A.

Charlotte Wright
Ravi Wright
Allegra Wright

Press 53
Winston-Salem

Press 53, LLC
PO Box 30314
Winston-Salem, NC 27130

First Edition

Cover design by Diana Greene

Cover art, Copyright © 2015
by Allegra Wright, used by permission of the artist's estate.

All interior drawings Copyright © 2016
by Allegra Wright, used by permission of the artist's estate.

Photo credits
Cindy Wright, page xi Milo photo and 89
David Lerner, page 57 and 85
Grant Wright, page xi young Allegra photo, back cover beach photo
Richard Fig Cassidy, back cover author photo
Tiffany Chaney, page 41

Printed on acid-free paper
ISBN 978-1-941209-56-1

You do not know somebody loves you
until she sees how ugly you are when you cry

—Milo Wright

Contents

Introduction

My first inclination was to tell you everything about my child. Milo's story demands to be told but that's perhaps another book. I will tell you that Milo's pronouns of choice varied from masculine to feminine to neutral. I stuck with the neutral—hence the "they" and "their" references. If I slip it's only because some things are hard-wired in my brain and difficult to change. I worked really hard to use Milo, their chosen name over Allegra, the one we assigned (their words). Also, it may not be evident that Milo had cerebral palsy and had limited use of their right hand and generalized weakness on their right side. This condition definitely affected their relationship with their body. Oops, there I go on the road to everything.

This book is a compilation of Milo's poetry—written over an all-too-brief lifetime. Milo began writing as soon as they figured out how to string letters together to form words and continued writing until their unexpected death at age 24. The only periods devoid of writing were those when the depression was too oppressive or the mania wouldn't allow cohesive thoughts.

Much of this work is autobiographical. Other pieces describe characters from one of their plays or an inspiration derived from a song, a book, or an insight gained from a unique perspective of the world. The writing reflects struggles with a myriad of health issues, a fluid gender identity, and a tumultuous succession of friendships, loves, and losses.

As Milo's mother, and a fellow writer, I had the privilege to share in the writing process. We would bounce around ideas, offer critique and push each other to persevere and finish. Early on, my greatest challenge was getting Milo to save work. I can't tell you how many spiral notebooks I found lying around with hunks of pages ripped out and thrown away. Occasionally, I would find these in time to fish a few sheets from the trash and stash them away in a hidden file. There are more than one of these gems in this book.

For the last few years, Milo began to see the value in their writing beyond what they gained from just getting it out. The impact their words had on others became apparent. More was saved, edited, and typed. A couple of months before they passed, Milo created a file of edited poetry. We had been planning to make this book together.

In our family, we say you always need to be ready with Plan B. Plan A was to work in earnest on this collection after my short story collection was launched. Milo helped me write some promotional blurbs. Along the same vein, my New Year's resolution was to follow through on positive ideas and inclinations.

March 20th of 2016, at around 4:00 a.m., I received a phone call. It was David, Milo's partner. He said the paramedics needed to speak to me. Milo was unresponsive. They had done all they could to revive them. We found out a few days later that the cause was an undetected heart defect. After all of the hard work, battling paralyzing depression, a battle they were beginning to win, this came out of nowhere.

In the days that followed, I came up with Plan B. The book had to be completed. These words are treasures. For me, because they are actual thoughts, feelings, and insights written by my child who is no longer here. Many of these poems I heard read aloud from a stage, over the phone, or while snuggled together on the couch. Others I read while Milo stood by, examining my face for a response. Through these words, those memories are more viable. When I am reading them, I can often hear her voice or see her animated face and bent hand pounding out a point.

For you, the reader, I believe they can be treasures as well. Read carefully and thoughtfully and you will gain understanding of the issues addressed, and in a small way you will get to know Milo. What I hope you will learn from Milo is that life is worth the fight, even when the obstacles keep coming and seem insurmountable. Forgiveness is a process. Love isn't always pretty or happy and should never be taken for granted. Celebrate when you can. Don't assume that you and the person next to you are having the same experience or even seeing the same sights and hearing the same sounds. Unexpected turns often require unconventional responses.

Here's to follow through, Plan B, but most of all, here's to the wise, generous soul who is my beloved child.

Cindy—Milo's mom

This book is
to all
the poets
that wish
to
target the world
through poetry

Walking

Walking
Talking haveing
fun
jumping runs
jumper clothes
happy all day crazy day
that's how I like it!

Written in Ms. Kiser's kindergarten class

Just Me

I get around differently,
I maneuver things with intellect,
I set up things with my mind.
My brain keeps things,
My thoughts process things
my body does it all from my head.
My right side is weak,
But my dreams are strong.(The don't
train with Muhammad Ali.)
I started a service club,
Am swimming on high rank,
Beat my cerebral palsy,
and am living a great life
today.

Balloon

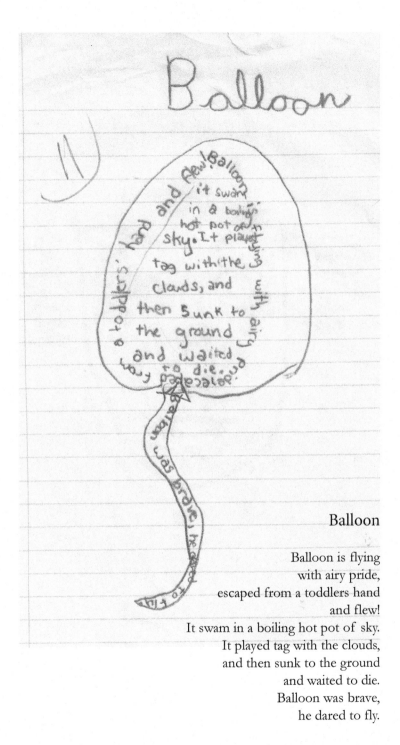

Balloon is flying
with airy pride,
escaped from a toddlers hand
and flew!
It swam in a boiling hot pot of sky.
It played tag with the clouds,
and then sunk to the ground
and waited to die.
Balloon was brave,
he dared to fly.

A series of Facebook wall messages I wish I could send

The dictator-ish physical therapist I had for too long:
Hello, Ms. So-and-So. How on earth did you think that telling a little disabled kid that they could "do anything if I try harder" would work? For your information, some fraction of me still believes that. Some scared little thing wants to know when he's trying enough. Well, 17 years later, I'm decided: What we did wasn't worth it. Especially about the FUCKING SHOESLACES.

Fuck you. I will not tie my shoes, and when you make me kickbox that stupid huge punching bag, I'm trying my damnedest with my quivering little disabled lower body to kick and punch it as if it's your face. I'm trying hard to this very DAY.

But really, as it stands, I'm not going to try to tie my shoes again before I'm ready, so fuck off. If I need pep talk to get me through something else, mind what you say.

Aftermaths

I rip the phone from its charger and escape upstairs
I am Dorothy in the tornado
I can hear the howling winds around me
panic in my stomach
completely alone with myself and my racing mind.
The house is silent.
I find the body-shaped wrinkles of the comforter I fit into.
I burrow.
Into the cocoon I go.
I grimace
and yelp in pain.
The sweeping cuts have not yet dried
they still hurt when touched.
They are red.
I reach for the phone with a tiny T-rex arm
and dial with shaky hands.
"Hello?" she answers, wide awake, eager. "Oh no. What's wrong?"
"I did it again."
She gasps, swallows, but maintains
her over-the-phone poker face.
"Are you okay?"
Her voice spills out over me
concerned and soothing like a cool hand
on a hot forehead.
I whisper.
"I guess. At least I can hide it."
I wince again
I shudder.
It hurts, it hurts . . .
"I'm trying to stop."
She recoils and tries a different tactic.
"I love you."
I smile, albeit with difficulty.
"I love you too."
I feel warmth in her motherly tone
something sincere.

"It is NOT a setback
just a challenge. Do you hear me?
You are GOING to get better.
You can!"
I close my eyes and exhale
as she talks me down
from my alarm.
"Thank you." I sigh
and hang up.
It's dark outside
Something in me wonders why
I deserve this sort of pain.
Something else snarls and grins at the same time.
Was it enough?
Who knows anymore?
Who knows?
I just want it to stop.
I want to feel good.
I want to be a girl.
I want to just be a girl
a girl who knows how to love herself.
I don't know how.
The eager little voice in my head
reminds me: you are.
I run to the bathroom and begin
the grueling process
of cleaning my wounds.
I use rubbing alcohol, gauze, Band-Aids, Neosporin
and an unhealthy dose of guilt
to heal my scars.
I just want to be happy.
As I apply the Neosporin
it hits me hard.
Well, why not start?

Childhood Prompt

Dinner that night was spent with me silent and swollen faced
reality being
that my life was over as I knew it
settling over my narrow little shoulders
a video tape of teenage faces twisting in disgust and fury
rewound and played
rewound and played
I almost wanted to return to the car rider pickup behind my school
and see
if my best friend's spit that had been carefully
aimed for me
and missed
was burning a hole in the pavement
with its venom
the endless rumbling silence
of a hundred gossiping children
watching the death of a soul
and the war cry of a girl who smelled like bubblegum
and had me on a fight list in her back pocket
"IT'S CAUSE SHE'S A LESBO! LESBO!"
echoed in my skull and through the stairway to my room
like famous last words at a public execution
until I jammed my headphones on and pressed play
and everything except the opening note
was silence
the kind that had been missing since the days
of swimming in amniotic fluid.
I laid in bed as still and fragile as an ICU patient
a voice like heartbreak come to life
pumped the poison from my stomach.
I fell deep asleep, and my mind was as blank and dark
as a wet chalkboard
until I began to dream:
It was another school morning, getting ready in the bathroom.
in SHE walked, stark naked, dried spittle
still in the corners of her smirking mouth, eyes crazy

as she drew a bath, and stepped in. I felt ill.
I shuffled out of the bathroom with eyes downcast
and ran smack
into HIM.
the man with the voice like heartbreak come to life was standing
RIGHT THERE.
He knelt down and wrapped me up in his arms
his hair a velvet curtain all around me, all muscle and warmth
his impish smile pressed against my ear . . .
I awoke to my alarm's unpleasant buzz
still wearing headphones
and noticed something was a little different . . .
But what?
As I got up, my insides were open and airy, afloat.
I pushed play again and as the music made my room pulse
I was pushed back down.
Suddenly I remembered
"Everyone at school hates me . . ."
But as I stood and selected the day's clothes
inside began
a tiny rebellion.
"So fucking what?"
My mind bloomed
into outright treason. "Let them.
Let them call me a bitch
a freak
a muff-diving
girl-chasing
faggot.
LET THEM.
I'm the biggest, baddest, craziest dyke warrior princess they've ever
seen. LET *them* be afraid. Let them think I'm poison. This dyke
warrior princess can't be killed by something as petty as hate. Let
them try. Go ahead. Beat me with a bible, yell, spit, cuss, perform
an exorcism! I'm ready."
As I walked into school to face my peers,
I was high as a kite on my own power, full of joy
realizing without a doubt
that I was meant to survive.

Silicia

The smell of unknown algae
from the lake house
you didn't make it to
(you lost weight, you were sick, your mother says you're sorry)
was hovering
around my head that
Sunday morning
as I tamed
the fresh scruff
sprouting from my head
and smudged
kohl all around
my eyes.

It wasn't until
I stabbed my eye
with the
eye shadow sponge
and a lone tear coated in black slid down my face
like some cliché movie poster
("I just wanted to be big, and sad, and loved, just like her")
that I heard your voice in my head.
"God, that's so emo. We should sell you to Hot Topic on a t-shirt."
(girlish giggles, elbow elbow, nudge nudge,
pantomiming our angst-ridden icons like saints)
and it hit me what kind of day it was
I felt so sheepish just then
the feeling stayed the whole drive there
should have known
when I saw you your smile
was a little crescent greeting me
but you smiled.

The closer I looked,
the more your smile
matched your body

a pale, sharp little crescent
floating through the world as if
it wasn't in it anymore
(isn't there a song about just that?
About the way you look right now?)
(Shit. It's gotta be somewhere in my Ipod.
Who sang it?? What's the title??)
I don't remember much about that hour or two or a few
except your hugs were tight and you
still
weren't afraid to look me in the eye
even though my own storm had started.

I could be scary to look at
your hugs were tight
and your face slowly set the
same way it did when you started a new drawing
and that was what I held on to that day
while we listlessly wandered
your hugs were tight and your face read concentration
so even though we were a movie cliché, so slow pulling apart from
one another as you got in the car to get ready
I knew you'd be okay.
(She's gonna be okay. She's gonna be okay.
This isn't the movies. She isn't Angelina Jolie.
Oh, look, there's the song I couldn't remember.
Actually, there's two. Both sung by girls. No coincidence.)

I called you a few days in.
Your voice was shaking
as you told me how weird it was
but I still had that face in my head, and I knew you were okay.
For some reason, the first week you were gone
I kept stabbing myself in the eye with the eyeliner sponge
like my motor movements never wanted to forget
(the pain a firm stab followed by a flinching
fluttering escape into a bath towel. FUCK! QUIT IT!)
but I had to remember that face
and that your hugs were tight.

I called you while you were about to come home
and your voice was a chorus of excitable windchimes
as you told me about your new love for hot chocolate
and about happy colors and group therapy
I couldn't help but tell you "you sound amazing"
as the little crescent from the bookstore
grew wider and wider in my mind
(See!! Told you! Now how about you get yourself fixed?)
and then I knew you were okay
when your voice hugged me tight as you said
"I've been on an adventure!"

Death in Parts

an Introduction

People do some very strange things
when faced with potential or real death
of any kind, even if there is no corpse as proof
there are no two faces the same, or voices either
but how they twist and raise in reaction to an absolute end
is primal, something that not even cellphones and concrete
can take away from us.
When I see a death, I freeze
I shrink back with either my body or my mind and pull away
detaching like subcutaneous tissue from the epidermis
creating a blister that I then have to protect with my life
lest it be rubbed wrong or touch anything at all
and weep pus and never quite heal right.
There are a few death scenes I've witnessed
that left blisters
some have been left alone
to this day are still perfect little bubbles of hurt
others broke, reformed elsewhere, and broke again until
I began collecting keloids like spare change or seashells.

First

My freshman year
my best friend at the too-crowded high school I attended
was the kind of girl who broke everyone's heart
with how strangely beautiful and how utterly crazy she was
loved every vice you could love
from frequent sex to cigarettes to dum-dum lollipops
and we loved her even though we were her theatre
for her self-destruction as performance art
somehow she stayed alive
until her mom died
her maybe-girlfriend

pantomiming hanging herself in the cafeteria window
to tell us
and when the orphan herself came back
her hair was pink and more vibrant than her eyes
which were faded like
the pair of jeans you finally have to throw away
and so began her love affair with opiates
but the color in her eyes was gone for a long while.

Second . . .

Poetry for Her

Well, if you're looking for me to
cast my eyes down and
grin apologetically for
taking up space,
you aren't gonna get it.
Like
I know my body is a
rulebreaker
and it's not my place
to cater to your anxiety.
It's not my place to
assure you I'm not broken
or crazy
because I just might be both.
You're gonna have to learn
how to look me in the eye anyway
Look, I didn't have one of those childhoods
where the sun shone all the time
and I never broke a bone
or had my heart stepped on.
If you're looking for a charming
saccharine dateline special on
the triumph of the human spirit
where I tell you that anyone
can do anything
if they just try
look elsewhere
because I can't provide you
with things like that
and you might as well
go get validated
off of an inspirational
YouTube montage because
that's not who I am
it's not that simple.

(untitled)

There was the one night after *The Vagina Monologues*
when I was dizzy and reeling and flustered and proud
and I went up to hug you
your hair disheveled your face red your tie undone
from the effort of inciting riot for the night
and the space between the buttons of your shirt
was just big enough for my imagination
to crawl in
and ever since that night
I've wanted to touch that pink ruche of skin
that is ever so slightly raised
on your
bare
chest
ever since that night, I have fantasized
about running my palm
over your paintstroke tattoo
and down to your scars that cradle your nipples
like old coals on a fireplace, praying for a spark
and
lingering on their texture and
walking my fingers around from there
exploring the ebbs and flows it takes
to travel to your navel and the waistband of your
skintight jeans
but always going back
to the ruched skin with roughness beneath
trying my best to smooth it with coaxing strokes
that leave little earthquakes in their path
taking note of your pulse
that loves to gallop
at the slightest touch
or sweetest word
I have fantasized
about the sudden roadbump of your hipbone and
what it would feel like against my forearm

and the trails your ribs would make
to take me there
whether your ass would tilt to unite with my hand as we
try to be casual
walking down the street
saying hello to a cashier or barista
I wonder what your hands
would feel like
placed somewhere other
than my back or shoulder
maybe my stomach at first
and then wherever the wind blew
what would your earth hand
do with my fire hand
I wonder
but for now
first
I want to kiss you just once
just for starters
very quickly in
the heat of the moment
and have it end with
both of us blushing and apologizing
but
wondering what comes next
our synapses screaming
let's go again!
let's go again!
my hands quivering with wanderlust
for the space between your buttons
only big enough for my
imagination to crawl inside.

Calvin

I saw you, but
if you saw me see you
you gave no sign
too busy negotiating
with ghosts
clinging to your
beautiful boylashes
and bleeding into
your retinas
I would guess
I saw the unbrushed
jungle of hair
and the recent cuts
gashes
deep all up your forearms
and the
dripping eyeliner
and the
distant stare
and I thought
No, NO
this is the babbling remnant
of some demonic sacrifice.
Not my high school comrade.
Where is he?
Where is the little boy
with the Shirley Temple ringlets?
He was last seen in a Nirvana t-shirt
blue flannel button up, Tripp pants with chains and bondage buckles
and red high-tops.
He carries a marbled glass bowl and
black messenger bag with him at all times.
He can usually be found
charming one of the Goth sisters
by singing The Cure in a pretty warble.
I'm still looking Calvin

but I don't know if you'll come home.
As you smoked
your hands shook
your eyes moved in REM sleep
and you shouted misfits lyrics
at the bus engines.
I'm SORRY that I and
your opiate-addict, pink-haired orphan girlfriend
left in such a hurry.
She went to rehab.
I went to therapy.
And you, I don't know
where you went.
You were my friend
the sweet little stoner who mediated
between me and the
whole wide damn scary world
but now it seems the scary world
has almost scared you to death
certainly out of your wits
screaming Misfits songs at screeching bus tires
and yelling to your ghosts and Frankensteins
shaking as you smoke
you have lost whatever
sweetness you had
baby, you're no longer faded
but you're definitely burning
burning down.
I suppose it's appropriate
you were last seen in a Nirvana t-shirt.

Altarback

I woke up too late this morning
and realized
when I met you
I knelt down before you
when you showed me
what looked like kindness
my eyes dripping
knees scabby
heart pressing into concrete
and oozing fresh
and allowed you
to build an altar
on my paper white
skeletal
adolescent back
the altar of
The One Good Decision I Made

After that moment I never
learned that it
was crucial I sew my chest closed
I gushed all over you
not realizing
you relished the taste of
raw heart juices on your fingers
my little girl soul ached for
someone willing to
get their hands gory
so when you hung scales and idols
from my ribs
and burned incense and candles
on my spine
I thought it was
reverence
for my suffering

that I was an altar
meant I was precious

I never wanted to toss judgment
on you for the way you ticked
and the way you steered
my body and soul
but there comes a point
in every illness
where you should realize
abnormal chemical makeup
should never bleed into your persona
and that there is a
difference between
the narratives your brain passes as reality
and the reality that everyone
awakens to
that is composed of common sense and
dictates that you contribute
I do not blame your sick parts for lying to you
putting those nonsense rules all around
placing the distorted expectations
of your illness
on a world that clearly
doesn't work that way when healthy
I just blame you for believing

From the moment I met you
you were the kind of person
who molded her world
to fit her sickened needs
like a Lego set, or an open market
with baubles and sweet smelling tributes
I know this now
but until a few days ago
I maintained the growing piles of
offerings on my back like they were
my responsibility—

I did have a part in
fostering your twisted parts
that's over.
These offerings are
sticky and rotten
requiring a good scrub brush
but I will clean this mess you made of my body.

(untitled)

"The system is broken, Allegra," she says
"I know," I say
And unfortunately
it's easy to see
why I know so well
cos the school system
it's putting us through all the paces of hell
Yeah it's easy to see
the system's victims
You can see who they are in their eyes
You can hear who they are in their sighs
The school systems victims
Are the ones stuck in school at 21
Losing their cool on a daily basis
The school system's victims
Are the thirteen year old queers
that are tortured for years
by their peers
their weapons of choice?
Gym:
Basketballs
Footballs
Kick balls
and other forms of instruction.
The school system's victims
Are the silenced students
          and activists
Spitting the truth in class
But as these things come to pass
          these boys and girls, still sucking their thumbs
          the first time they sang "we shall overcome"
Are censored but their words
are triumphant
And they still spit tenacious venom
in coffee shops like this
and bedrooms
and mosh-pits

Memory from the Smoking Patio
at Krankies, 2010 or 2011

She did not fade
she was definitely burning
she was picked clean by starvation and arrythmia
leftovers, ashes with a few sparks left inside
a Shakespearean tragedy flayed open but left on the bone
for all the vultures of the world
she was gorgeous...
a flame redhead with
a Greek nose
Spanish lips
and Scandinavian eyes
she smoked Marlboro reds and drank Americanos
black. She shook from heroin and alcohol and cold
quivering in the way an arrow does
before being shot from its bow
all the time.

She wore a knee-length black leather jacket and
Knee-high red Doc Martens
Oh . . . she was gorgeous . . .
she played piano but didn't sing
Even though I begged her to
even though her larynx was aching to
even though it would have saved her . . .
and
she called me babygirl . . .
babygirl . . .
a word never used before nor since.
I have never known a diminutive term to sound so
assertive, like I had finally become somebody's
knight-princess in shining armor
like by her saying that word
I was going to be the assassin for any and all
demons for her,
like babygirl was the passkey to the castle.

Oh God she was gorgeous.

Her hands were long and elegant
but held my shoulder with death's grip to steady herself
and I imagined death's grip held hers the same way
digging fingernails into her clavicle like an ill-fitting pet collar.
I made a point to hold her gently
as her little girl body with little bird bones
stumbled and shivered and smoked and got stuck
and her heart kept beating so WRONG
under her shrieking, sharp ribs
so wrong, so broken, so sick

and the last time I saw her face, with her
Greek nose
Spanish lips
and Scandinavian eyes
I thought it funny
funny-sad, not funny-silly
that I loved her so much in two dates
more than I ever loved anyone
in two dates
the pit of my stomach burned with the knowledge
that every time I saw her might be the last time
but she was still a treasure and I still loved her
I prayed that night that she'd be okay, come back from the dead
and then the next day I called her
called her twice, three times, four
voicemail
and then she disappeared for three years only to
reappear in my text inbox for three months only to
go away again until the present day
those three months over text made me think she was okay
getting better
but then she was gone again.

I still love her
composed more of memory than reality
I'd love to call her and see what happened

but the truth is
I'm afraid that my starving, arrhythmic, vice-loving babygirl
is just another instance of me
falling in love with the undead and the dying
I'm afraid that if I try to find and love her one more time
I'll just have another martyr to remember
just another patient who never recovered
just another leftover story that flits behind my eyelids
in hazy daydreams and putrid nightmares
I'd love to call her and see what happened
but her memory is so beautiful I'd hate to spoil it
If only I had the courage to burst this bubble and realize
she's probably gone
Do I try?
Oh God, she was gorgeous . . .
Do I try?
Oh, Oh God, she was gorgeous . . .

That One Time I Learned to Say "I Love You!"

That one time I learned to say
"I love you"
(Or was it the second or the third?)
I was pressed between layers
of people and their hearts
kitchen smells and off-color walls
of hot and of cold.
I had forgotten the embraces
that filled days past
+ I was the mohawked, skinny white girl
sitting off to the side terrified.
I knew I was in theory
loved here
but didn't know what exactly
this feeling in my stomach was, then came
the feeling of a hand on my
back
pressing me into the mix
and out it came
"I love y'all."
That day I learned the fundamental
rules of community with Jesus in mind
1. Hang w/ all the wrong folks.
2. If someone isn't mad @ you and yours,
you aren't quite doing it right.
3. Love without a fence.

Seeping into my skin and running down my body
this hospitality was the solvent that
concocted three words
with
sincerity
I love y'all.

And the more you practice
hospitality
the easier it comes out from
between your lips
I love y'all.

What To Expect When You're Abruptly Expecting

It's December 2012. Advent and the End of Days are underway.
It would seem that two such events would be bookends
on the timeline that is diagrammed on our breastbones.

Humans carry a story in their skeletons
that is unerasable. A strange effort
of narration told in many tongues,
almost as explicit as our DNA sequences, the words constantly
unzipping themselves, multiplying, dividing, deciding our fate.
In the past, we listened. It was our survival manual. We read the
messages inscribed within us like a sacred code
because they were, back then. They were what made us run when
we were chased, comfort when others were hurt, and sing when we
felt moved to sing.
They whispered the mandatory instinctive tricks that we wouldn't
understand without learning first.
And now we don't need them, our bone scriptures,
because we have
things much better, and faster-moving
than legend, poetry, proverb, or story.
We stopped following the call
that put our feet in the dirt in the first place.

So of course the intersection of Advent and the End of Days
comes as a surprise.
It only makes sense that an double dose ass-kicking
must be delivered by the calendar
to drill through the litter of a progressive society.
That only a scheduled interruption can interrupt our schedule.

Our ancestors are laughing through their tears.

Advent and the End of Days may seem like bookends,
because how can the world burn before rebirth?
Advent and the End of Days are linked today because
they command the same requirements.

Advent says, "Watch, wait, listen, anticipate,"
and the End of Days says, "Watch, wait, listen, anticipate."
At last, the story in our skeletons gets to exercise its voice again.
The whisper in our bones has always commanded us:
"Watch, wait, listen, anticipate."
And now the calendar year, our master, boss, and leader,
is synced with our instinct and a sense of the holy.
Unfortunately,
now is the time everyone is going to panic
as if we're cramming for some exam
or have left the oven on and the deadbolt unlocked at home.
While some of us have chosen the path of hopeful skepticism and
optimistic anticipation, this is an ideal time for the sensationalism
to sneak in the back door and work its way through the nail-biting
masses leaving heart palpitations, depersonalization episodes,
and overcompensating acts of overconfidence in its wake.

I can't even escape sensationalism's havoc on the bus.
Two women beside me talk with unabashed sureness about
"the state of things."
One holds a book unimaginatively titled
Escaping the Devil's Grip,
the other compulsively pulling at her scarf,
untying it, taking it off, and knotting it around
her neck again.
Cue scene:
"I'm getting sick and tired of this torn-up world."
"Oh, yes, there just isn't 'nough morality to go 'round anymore."
"Honey, you know, I'm just waiting for the Rapture."
"Waiting for Jesus. Yes ma'am, you can see it coming already!"

A couple of counterpoints materialize in my mind.

1. Do you really think the Mayans and Israelites have been in on
    this together all along? I mean, have the two groups held strategic
    meetings while Jesus was maturing and the calendar was being
    carved? Like, co-coordinating schedules, brainstorming ideas for
    the halftime show to the End-Times? Example—"Hey, Mayans,
    Jesus said it was cool if we scheduled Judgment Day before his
    birthday. You gonna be ready by then?"

2. Is looking up your only concern? Have you given the least bit of thought to the roots of Earth's apparent lack of morality? Has your whole life consisted of shaking off the desperate and the lost surrounding you, your eyes cast to the breaking clouds obviously meant for you alone? You can't live life with tunnel vision to the clouds. You are not the only person on Earth. Your purpose on earth is not to earn a space in the sky, ready for you to be sucked up and make a home upstairs.

I awkwardly meet their eyes for a moment and realize
I likely look like
a Mad Max model of immorality and survivalism
a couple weeks too early.
I walk among them, over-prepared.
A reverse anachronism.
A chronological misfit who already knows
what to pack, including weaponry, clothing, and food,
how to live like you're the only survivor left,
and where to hide when you fail.
It's true, in my time the End of Days has come and gone
once or twice. It played out
behind my eyelids and under the bedclothes,
on the street and in the desert.
I know exactly what it looks like.
And this one may not come. The End of Days
has bought time and held off a few times already.
And if this one is late too, I'll wake up on the 22nd
with Monday still coming.
If it's time, and my guesses are outright wrong?
I'll swallow what I've said here, but I won't panic.
I'll open the shades and welcome the Lake of Fire and waves
of eternal destruction facing forward,
Just like the last time my world came to an end.

Suicidal I

I like to think
I drew a rune of protection on you
with the grease from my hair
built up
from the
three showers I didn't take
since that night.
I see that each of the
130 resentful words you sent me
were proof
that your hands could still type.

I want to think that
the breaths I didn't breath
in the moments
I was praying for guidance that day
when I wasn't praying much these days
traveled straight to your lungs and
kept you going
when not much else would.
These are miracles I can work with.

I believe these things sincerely
and whether or not
you see them as a blessing is
nothing I care about.
I just wanted you in the right hands
and whether you know it or not
you are. My wish was granted.

Suicidal II

It's my bedtime
and I should be doing
only one of two things:
brushing my teeth
staring blankly
in the mirror, taking my pills
and sleeping
or writing
what I
intended to write
and staying up
all night
drinking and eating
instead
I'm desperately clawing
at your name on the
computer screen
and wishing so bad that
those words that strike
the fear of god in me
didn't keep popping up
so much.
So no sleep, no
actual work done
just eyes screwed open
watching the girl who I
worshiped in high school
all the way from her
multicolored hair
to her plaid blazer to her Converse
fall to shreds
over a grocery list of things
I didn't quite grasp.
And all I want to say is
"I'm sorry"
but it's like shouting into space.

Harder

Dear you,
I'm thrilled to death that I had the honor
of making everything worse for you.
I suppose I did make everything worse
I certainly made it harder. That's how this thing called living can be.
Your everything, before I ruined it, was simply a question of when
and a question of how.
When: tomorrow, this weekend, 14 days, or tonight?
How: a bottle of Tylenol, a string of scarves, or a kitchen knife?
You would have thought that 2000-2014 was a nice even epitaph
and then you would never
have to think again. But no, I just ruined it.
I made you stay. I can't make you recover, but
I'll shout out across every phone and ethernet line
in this city to make you stay.
I hope to God Almighty that you choose to use
your bought time to get better
but seeing as I made everything worse
my hopes and dreams don't matter.
That's okay. They don't have to matter.
I put you in the right hands
stepped away, and they caught you.
Yes, this weird mistress called Death
is an easy creature to court, I know.
Her bastard, wide-eyed felon son. Life is
not easy to love. But you've got at least a little
more time to get to know him.
Yes, in a way I did make everything worse, but damned
if I did and even more damned if I didn't.
You know what would have made everything worse?
Your mother finding you.
Your mother ordering a coffin with blank eyes and pale skin.
Your father wondering why he wasn't there.
Your father referring to you as his "late daughter."
Your best friend flying up from Mexico
in black lace with stiff shoulders.

Your best friend running into your room, and burying
her face in your band shirts
as if to give you one last hug.
Your other best friend going catatonic from shock.
Your other best friend never returning to your hometown
because she knows too many people who knew you.
Your theatre colleagues turning to each other with nothing to say.
Your theatre colleagues destroying their careers with vodka and pot
to make memories of you go away.
And me . . . yes . . . me.
Me staring at your gravestone
wondering why the numbers on it are so even
and so goddamned small.
Me wishing you made it to New York.
Me regretting that I never told your mom that you were scaring me.
That would have made everything a hell of a lot worse.
I'm not ashamed. You're alive.
The rest of the work is yours to do.
I hope you get to it soon.

In Which Milo Became Exactly the Kind of Preachy Adult That They Have Grown to Hate

Okay.
Hey, honey, you're only seventeen, pay attention.
You did not get assigned the exact life you wanted.
Shame, shame.
Everything should fall into place.
You wanted to have
an agreeable life
but
life threw you to the pavement
skinned your knees
and everyone tells you
"you should feel lucky"
with a body that you yourself fear touching
much less having someone else do it
a mother who doesn't open her mouth
except to tell you how sick you are
peering in your room and spitting at your one therapy
writing—
and never touching you
except with a hand
forking out cash for your
only real getaway
twisted sticky white wrapper
with a cherry on top
a religion that hasn't touched you so much
as tried to shake sense into you.

Hey, honey, you're only seventeen, pay attention.
The two of us ended up
a little different.
I fought for a long time,
and spoiler alert!
Yes, you are allowed to feel cheated,
but fighting and mourning wastes energy

you could use. If you go on like that too long
next comes
depressed
isolated
resentful
handfuls of pill
lung full of smoke
and throat full of drink doing
Nothing. At all.

Hey, honey, you're only seventeen, pay attention.
No, you were not born
with the body you wanted.
No, you were not born with the family that really knows you.
No, you were not born with a brain that always
does what it should.
No
No
and No.
That fucking sucks.
From one skinned-knee vagrant to another
I'm sorry.

Hey, honey, you're only seventeen, pay attention.
You are smart
and very kind
and sweet, and
you have a lot
you can use for good.
You have more steps to endure,
but more effort doesn't mean it's not worth the try.

Hey, honey, you're only seventeen, pay attention.
What's a waste is an amazing kid like you
shooting down
a spiral of self-hate
never leaving your room again.
What's a waste is not working
for what you deserve.

Hey, honey, you're only seventeen, pay attention.
Yes, your path,
and my path,
is turny and twisty
and seems, to quote you
"utterly fucked up"
but it's a start.
Take a deep breath,
leave your worrying at the door
and go.
Or else you end up left in the doorway.

Gingerbread Manifesto

Love songs and Christmas music on the radio
Bring new meaning to the phrase
"Happiness is a warm gun"
Wish I had one sometimes
To blow holes in that radio
Not because I'm cynical
But because things like good cheer are over done
And besides, I've gotten nowhere fast
Believing that everything will be okay
Because, HAH! It won't.
But in its own fucked up way
in being not okay
Things can turn another direction
That might not be the best one
But at least that direction has an open end
And even more directions to turn into
Happiness may be a warm gun
But joy is realizing
(before it's too late)
that you must
STOP
what you are doing
Go down another road
Do not pass go or collect $200
That joy is finding the weeds and clipping them
So that they do not choke
your trees and flowers
when you realize that nothing is really
Really
Permanent
And instead
You have a choice
of changing your
path
That path will shift
before you

And will become
What
You want it to be and
along comes reality
as you see it.

Writer

I'm the girl who'll cry buckets
and quickly pull out her notebook
as wet words fall in her lap
to catch them.

Tailgating Fate

Limping on a leg
that is no longer mine
to the homeland
that is my favorite
coffee shop
I realize
I am
tailgating fate
too blind to succumb
to the current
paradigm
too stubborn
to explain myself
I must become
bigger than my body
(and up yours, John Mayer)
but it's true
I may lose a foot
or two of height
but I will be bigger
and yes, I talk too much
and don't do much else
but I am no de-beaked
chicken
send home from a factory
farm
I am a loving fighter
wielding sisterhood
and the handheld control of life
like a twin light saber
a twin light saber plucked
from the grimy paws
of Darth Maul
glowing red
red like the blood
that makes women

and other heroes fight while
tied together
I have mentioned previously
I ain't no working-class hero
but I am willing to work
and if hero comes
along, so be it
I'll take the title
use it
to my advantage

Chelsea Grin,
She's Got a Problem

She rocks forward and back
from her hips and ankles
like a shadow puppet whose strings
are suddenly snatched by new hands.
When she moves, she stretches like an old tomcat
her cavernous stomach curling even further in
and her vertebrae appearing below the skin like piano keys.
When she does her best to smile
her luxurious lips pull back and to either side
never curling up delicately like little girls are commonly taught
so it's more of a Chelsea grin than delicate laughter.

She greets you with that smile now as you
sit down across from her
her sparkling hungry eyes clouded with kohl
and powder, the skin of her hands taut around her teacup
ending in beetle-black fingernails.
You love her so much, she's your darling, your sweetie pie
your favorite girl
but this, this is it.
You know that you were last on her farewell list.
You know, but you try really hard to smile
the way you wish she would as she chatters on and on.

Your girl is trying to make you believe
that what you know to be true
is a lie.
No, this isn't goodbye, this is a hello
a real hello, nice to see you, how are you, I miss you
I love love love you, hello.
But tomorrow she's going away for a while to get better
like you can't
and you know she's gone after that.

She hangs on tight to her Chelsea grin as you bring her
in to hold her.
She'll never cry in front of you
never ever. Somehow she's always made it so
that you cry before she does.
And so you hold her, and you realize that you
never wrote her good enough poetry, and
that you could never compete with a fix.
Your words were never good enough to
make her sigh like she did when she began to nod
and you're sorry that now she has nothing new to sigh for.

Dear Earthlings,

Care Of/Attention—misguided social media commentators, bus
seat hoggers, ignorant board of trustees members, inspiration porn
consumers, Big Pharma conspirators, and you shitty parents who
stare at me but tell your poor, curious, confused children not to,
sit down.
Shut up.
Give me a moment of your time.

It has come to my attention that you have never, ever
talked to a disabled person before
except to tell us how BRAVE we are
for not shutting ourselves in the house
or to APOLOGIZE that we
were BORN this way, or better yet
to spout bullshit you learned
about us from Google and make suggestions
on how we ought to live our lives
based off of
FUCKING WIKIPEDIA.
So, Earthlings . . . HELLO.
I come among you
in peace. Though I am an odd
malformed creature
SO unlike you, I mean you no harm.
I come on behalf
of my sick and disabled fellows.
Don't worry.
I'm used to speaking for ALL of us.
Dear foolish, beautiful, tiresome earthlings
my people see
hear, and
feel your incrimination
EVERY DAY!
You look to us for proof
your life isn't so bad
you paste motivational quotes across our faces

and hang us on your mind's wall.
Hey, at least you're not
ANYTHING like me!
Your spine is straight
all four of your limbs work
and your brain is 100% NORMAL.
Thank GOD, right? You tell us
you could never do
what we do . . . smile
hold our head high
shop for groceries
and go on dates
DISABLED? No, you NEVER COULD.
God gave us this journey and made us special
because we can handle it . . .
well, until we can't, but that's not table conversation, is it?
And yet, despite all of this chatter
about our bravery, you make our lives
HARDER. Slam doors in our faces
park in our parking places
sit in our designated seats, and
verbally berate us when we're moving too slow
or taking up too much space.
And, Dear Earthlings, I feel no shame in explaining
what you know about us is prepackaged fluff.
No
we're not exaggerating
OR faking it, so give us the goddamn bus seat
before our knees collapse.
Yes
we need these big scary pills and constant doctor visits
to survive whether your tarot spreads and old gods
or Jenny McCarthy or Facebook friends
or whatever agree or not.
No
you can't touch our hands, face, cane, OR wheelchair.
No
it is not our bodies or brains that are a curse
it's a world that won't put elevators on a college campus

because it's historic, a world that tells us to stop whining
when we're in pain, a world that is totally fine with a book
titled *Crippled America* displayed in Costco
but not with me reclaiming it and throwing it lovingly in their faces.
Which brings me to my final point
Dear Earthlings, there is nothing BAD about our bodies
or our brains. A big scarlet "D"
was not tramp-stamped on us
as fetuses.
If your world learned not to fear us
we would not be reminded daily
of our constant struggle.
We COULD live in your world comfortably
if you let us
but NOOOO . . .
Dear Earthlings, I have been called
ET-phone-home
more times than I can count
but, Dear Earthlings, accept, for now
I am a part of your planet.
 Dear Earthlings, let me in.
Sincerely, the subject of your stares and whispers
a heroine
an alleged angel
a freak
a curiosity
a limp in the leg
a convenient permanent limp hand
your burden.

Sincerely
Milo, a perpetual Impossibility

(untitled)

I look in my mirror and I take a deep breath
The hardest thing for me to do now is admit this to myself
Cos I've wished for greener grass and I've felt the consequence
Rips and tears of a solitary mind which avoids common sense
I'm a new woman,
And not because I changed my address
Because secretly wanting to be free kept me trapped
I'm a NEW WOMAN cos my reflection said to myself
"Look in the mirror and take it all off
Everything you are and everything you're not
Lay it out on the floor.
There's no fighting the obvious anymore
You, you're a girl and you come from the south
Your body is not perfect, nor is the speech from your mouth
You've never fit in, but now you fit in your skin
The entire shape of you is a map of where you've been."
I look twice to see the reflection shift and dissolve back into me
I whisper to the mirror "Hello, good to see you again."
My likeness is me
this New Woman
As I look at this reflection that I've idealized
I've realized
I'm looking into this mirror with a smile

Happy

So now the poem is about me
and now we're both on equal ground
I have my voice, I have my choice
And I choose to sound like me
and have you
Yeah, I choose to sound like me
and have you
We can make our own summer
even though it's bitter cold
We can laugh and play like kids
And we'll never grow old
I want to sing the chorus
of my favorite song
and I want you to know the lyrics
even if you get them wrong
I want us to sit side by side
And I'll never tell a lie
You'll make me really happy
maybe till the day I die
I barely breath when the caller ID
reads your name
and you've made me happy sixteen
It'll never be the same

So now the poem's about you
and now we're both up in the air
You had your voice, you had your choice
And you chose to sound like you
and have me
Oh, you chose to sound like you
and have me
We can make it through this winter
even if the flowers are dead
We can walk up and down, hand-in-hand
With beautiful thoughts in our heads
I want to dance to the choruses
to all your favorite songs
and I want to try the steps
even if I get them wrong
I want us to sit by the lake
And you know I want this to stay
I make you really happy
Please be here today
I know you love
the way I talk
and indescribable feeling
please join me in this walk

Cabaret Bio 2

They all hit the porch and the lawn
practically eating their cigarettes.
Familiar faces . . .
I just didn't think it was us they needed.
North Carolina humidity puts a blanket on our shoulders
and the cricket chirps an affirmation
for our support group, as if saying, "Next turn, hon."
There are many faces hidden by hair
or faces hidden by eyeliner
or faces hidden by slumped shoulders.
We are family, the Beloveds that just needed a place to stay.
My brother's ex-girlfriend pulls
her fresh dye job out of her face and smiles wetly
"I never had a family, really, ever.
I never really stayed with anybody."
She launches across our huddle and squeezes me tightly.
"Thank you, Milo. I have somewhere to go."
Then another turn.
Oh, our Golden Age lookalike on three-inch heels.
This'll be good.
She spews several curses then shakes them off.
"I'm crazy. No, you guys don't get it. I'm waay crazy.
That's tough to like.
And I'm too much for people and man . . .
you guys. Bipolar is awful."
I frown. "Okay, who else has been casually called
or diagnosed crazy?"
Almost everyone raises their hand and starts a fresh cigarette.
The soft spoken boy in Toms and a toboggan chuckles.
"Ya'll are great. This is so great. I've never felt so safe."
"I've never felt so heard."
"I've never felt so at home."
"I've never felt so strong."
"I've never felt so motivated."
"I've never felt so smart."
"I've never felt so happy."

"I've never felt so taken care of."
"I've never felt so appreciated."
It's my turn.
"I've never felt so loved. Thanks, you guys."
We're silent, the heat surrounds us like a clamshell.
But then I realize: We missed someone.
She straightens, her banana-blonde hair
eating up the porch light and spitting out the moonlight.
Her voice is clear, as clear as the fact
that she's going to take over the world
and I approve.
"Hey you guys."
"Yeah?"
"There's so much I want to do in the world.
I just hope I can do it. You think I can?"
Another cricket saying, "Next turn, hon."
I clear my throat.
"I think we all can."

Chew, Chew, Swallow, Swallow

"Unintended food related consequences and casualties of my mental health decay."

*My father hands me my mother's leftovers. Her cooking is a work of art even when it's just the chicken and rice in front of me. Twenty minutes later, I've barely had any.

*He helps me clean out my fridge. A Tupperware of my mother's leftovers is several days out of date. I want to cry.

*Every time I take a bite of food these days I have to chant in my head "CHEW, CHEW! SWALLOW! SWALLOW!" to finish it, like I am a college freshman with Jager.

*I know how I can make this worse. I know how to shrink even faster, but I'm too cowardly to bite the bullet.

*I realize that my body won't feel the same to my goddaughter when I hold her, and she may learn to fear me because I'm so fucking sick.

*My impulse-driven buzz cut from months ago has barely grown, and I can't decide which wig to wear forever. I am a man who wants his hair.

*I now understand that they made up and dressed Angelina Jolie with biological and social accuracy. I know this because we're starting to look the same.

*My face is so dull and tired when I stare into it in the bathroom that I can practically hear a sandstorm blowing by and Bob Dylan trying with all his might to sound hopeful as he sings.

*My eyes have gotten so dark that nobody can ever know what I'm thinking again. It's not possible.

*My face fucking stings when I show emotion, like the lyrics to some song by some band 15-year-old me tried to like and couldn't.

*Unless it's after 11 p.m., solid food tastes disgusting. See above note on chanting like a college freshman to finish a meal.

*Apparently I'm beautiful and something to be envied now because I'm tiny and I've stopped raising my voice in public.

*My boyfriend has started bribing me with nutritional shakes in 18-packs from the drugstore where he works.

*My morning tea is double strong. I like the smell of cigarettes and dirty hair.

*I'm not sure what I actually look like.

Chew. Chew. Swallow. Swallow. Chew. Chew. Swallow. Swallow. And do not ever, ever cry where they see, lest you become performance art.

Honeylove

I heard "How Sweet It Is" on the radio today.
I wonder if James Taylor was in love
in a time of desperation
if he ever loved or was loved because
that was the only thing left in the moment.
I wonder if he has ever had to suck poison
from the lips of his lover
or rearrange the kitchen for her own safety
or soothe a scared panther until the shrieking stilled.
I would suggest to him that the sweetest love I have ever seen
was found somewhere terrifying—
I was loved even as my heart thrashed bitterly on craggy rocks
and my eyes and cheeks were salty swollen red.
The one I loved had my wrists and shoulders pinned between
her biceps, her triceps, and the bed pillows
and she was quiet
because all she knew was that I couldn't be alone that night
and that sex was the last of her worries
the last thing on her mind.
You do not know somebody loves you
until she sees how ugly you are when you cry
and responds immediately with an intervention
helping you into pajamas and into the kitchen chair with a
hot cup of tea
not resting until you smile again.
You do not know somebody loves you until you feel them
tuck themselves in behind you
her intentions not going anywhere beyond
wanting to rock you to sleep
and then gets up at two a.m. without waking you
to get rid of the sharpest razors and knives
and stashing them far away until the coast is clear.
You do not know somebody loves you until
they wake you up singing the Winnie the Pooh theme song
along with their smart phone
and clumsily making the coffee

so that the water spills everywhere
and you spend the first few minutes of the morning
wanting to roll your eyes
and hate this frivolity after such a long night
but then realize that it's because of her clumsy
gangly ways of loving
that you are so enchanted
and if she can do it again two years later and 500 miles away
you know you've got a winner.
So no, love is not always so sweet like honey
or calm and cool and palatable as some would make it out to be
but it's easy to spot
because once you have it it's the only thing you want.
A toast to those who do not love easily or sweetly
and to those who are loved that way
we salute you.
For once it's yours it's yours forever.

Blue Bottle

She pressed chapped lips to a blue bottle and tipped it back. Vodka swirled down her throat; she purred and took another drink.

Lips peeled over her teeth in a crooked smile, mouth exploded in a laugh, and head tilted back. Body separated from mind.

Her mind was gone, having packed its overnight bag, hoisting it over its shoulder and walking into the sunset.

She didn't want it.

Didn't want to think.

The alcohol washed away all the cobwebs from the corners of her skull and everything appeared pristine.

She didn't have to think.

She laughed again. And again. And again.

The world was a circus. Everyone should laugh *all* the time. Everything was so much better when you were laughing.

She leaned into the man next to her, resting her head on his shoulder, looping her arms around his waist. Why wasn't he laughing?

She dug her fingers into his white cotton shirt. He smelled nice. Like happy times. She nuzzled into the crook of his neck and took a breath.

He placed his hands on her forearms, uprooting her, and pushed her away.

                                        Why did he have to leave

Everyone always seems to leave.

She lifted the now empty bottle to her eye and squinted, looking through it.

Now everything was blue.

She didn't feel like laughing
anymore

(untitled)

They found her pacing 4th street
pulling her too-long hair
mumbling about "losing me."
I didn't have the heart to kill her
so I left her at the bar and sent her a text.
People keep chasing her down
dusting her off
and sending her to my house in a cab
and I keep ditching her
"Honey, I love you, but you don't make me
smile."
She's intent that cohabitation is possible
that sharing organs is no problem
but it's small in here
She ruins my appetite and makes me overthink myself
I can't just walk
just talk
just eat, drink, breath
I have to do it for her
As far as my friends go, they scarcely see her
she takes up too much room at the table
and doesn't say a word
just glares
so they look past.
She holds my hands too tight
I can feel her trying to shuffle and shake my brain
and suck me back in to her sick orbit
yes, she's possessive
trying to dollify a body that can't even stand straight
or maintain delicacy
I'm just never going to be like her
like she wants
I'm too crooked in every way
to be pretty like her
I'll never be straight or shapely enough
For now we make chase

and when she catches me we share
uncomfortable air
I am a sight to behold
The boy with a second head
and a second heart
but the same blood
Though she clings and morphs
to my every word and move
I do love her somehow.
Stand, my fellow patrons
witness and take note
of the boy fighting for space.
The world simply is not ready
for his body on its own.
She's starved him for years
prevented him from growing.
All he wants is to be
tall, narrow, and marble-carved
without the second head and heart
eating him alive and maintaining control.
Behold.
No, the world is not ready for such
a strange body without her behind it
but every bone, tissue, or patch of skin
will come hurtling forth to Earth
without her judgment call of value.
Someday, I'll be my own body.
Someday, she won't try to come home.

Eulogy for Ian Curtis

Your singing
was more like a plea
to the gods
reaching the rafters
and climbing over
the audience
in a frenzied cry.
The band raced
to keep up
glancing nervously
at each other
knowing that they
would fail to
do you justice
Watching your body
teeter before them
like a prisoner on
a coastal pirate ship
they were methodical
in their rhythm
while you battled
something just
beyond the stage.
I wonder, darling
if anyone in the audience
was saying their goodbyes
as they watched you
if anyone knew you were dying
right there before them
or could guess that
you had been locked in the bathroom
sick
right before you stumbled on stage
to state your case
to the demons concealed by spotlights.
Something about
the sound of your voice

I hear now
tells me I would have known
and I would have been misty-eyed
and alone in the crowd
with my worries.
But I was not there.
I saw nothing.
I can't say.
But I know this:
twelve years later I was born
and today
something about
the strangled yell in "New Dawn Fades"
at the last show
you ever did
rattles a part of my soul
that isn't touched much.
Something about your eyes
makes me feel like
I'm staring at myself
when I go to find you
on the web.
Something about
your dancing
makes me wonder
if I took your feet.
Something about
your hatred of interviews
the anxiety
the depression
the lack of control
and fear of the spotlight
later in life, rings harsh
in my ears.
And when I can't
catch my breath or I seize
in my dreams
it feels like something beyond me
is fighting to survive.
Darling, is that you?

Ashes

On Ash Wednesday, they projected a painting on the wall
and each little detail reminded me of a little piece
of your decay into sickness
I did very well at containing my tears
but as my eyes traveled, so did my mind
to every warning sign I missed from the moment I met you
ours was never a romance
but it was a love story for the ages
and like clay, like ash, deserves a proper burial.
I was angry at you. I was bitter. But now
I'm grieving.
First, I saw the gold flecks
and I remembered your hair on the floor.
The special kind of light that you only find at one a.m.
filtered into our little house like a secret too good to keep
out of the lips of a grade school best friend.
We were stressed and sallow, our laughter was tense and loud
like a teakettle whistle.
I had watched you fight with your father twice that day
on the phone, in the living room
and seen the first flickers of madness in your eyes.
That night, you dragged a kitchen chair into our bathroom
and handed me your beard trimmer
declaring that the sweet little boy your father had known
was gone, that you were sharpening your edges
and there were those flickers in your eyes again.
We shaved each other's heads ritualistically
purposely moving in time to the razor
so that my chest pressed into your back
and then your stomach met my shoulders as
our hair fell at one another's hands
as we squeezed each other goodnight
our hands traveled to the newfound skin and stayed there.
You kissed my forehead and said that this was the best fresh start
you could have asked for.
Next, I saw the ring around the outside

and remembered the black semicircles
that began to grow under your eyes
under your nails, under your cheekbones
and under the piles of unwashed dishes
all of which only seemed to grow in time
the angrier you got
the less you slept, showered, or shaved.
But the more you wanted to hold on to me
the more you wanted me there.
You were the king of crocodile tears
keeping me hooked into your saga.
We stayed up late every night consoling each other
even though it was us causing us pain
we were making each other crazy
but there was no other way
and if anyone asked
I said that for all of his new quirks
I needed him badly, and I was happy to have him.
I thought your desperation, stumbling walk
and fast talk were charming.
It made me feel worthwhile
even when you touched me
when I didn't want to be touched.
I didn't flinch.
I was proud to be one of the few you still let in.
It stayed that way for the longest time
but the black under your eyes, nails, cheeks
and sink kept getting darker
eventually sinking between your ribs
and I knew that you were being consumed
the man who told me he didn't love me anymore
was one big black smear.

Waltz with Apollo

As I dance for him
he tells me I am ample
and all is right in the world
and for once I enjoy filling space with
the waves and ripples of my body.
This body, he says, is a perfectly ripe pear
wrapped in cloud skin and painted with bits
of blue and red and honey brown.
It is worthy of loving
it is worthy of display
it is a celebration worthy of the gods
he says with a wry, knowing chuckle.

As I dance, he drinks it in slowly,
savoring my offering.
I am barefoot, my thighs
poured into jeggings like twin glasses of milk
whole fat milk
my breasts, as round as farmers market apples
in a lacy red underthing
and my stomach and hips can barely contain themselves.
They loosen to the toasty air
like the evidence of the adequate nourishment they are.
My scars blur with my movement into stretch marks.
He says, call them growing pains

As I dance, suddenly I feel him behind me
swaying my hips from side to side with his harp-player hands
the buttons of my spine line up with the path of his sternum
he nestles his chin in my softened shoulder
and he whispers

"You are crafted from earth
you are art whether you are at movement or at rest
if only you saw what I see of you
you chose me, but I choose you right back . . ."

and then he calls me by the name he chose for me
and when I finally pull myself out of this reverie
as the phone rings
I feel his words pounded into my heart
pulsing with each pump of vital blood

tonight, as I rub tea tree oil on my scars
and feel clumsy in my skin, I remember that night
I remember that this dull ache in my thigh
is just growing pains
that I am a perfectly ripe pear, that I am art
that I am celebration
and he strokes my scars and guides me
out of the bath
and firmly tells me

"Don't forget."

Stoic

I dreamed for years
of one day looking in the mirror
and being able to see right through the reflection
neutral
two eyes, a nose, lips, hair
all where they're supposed to be
a face, nothing to be afraid of
nothing to judge
nothing to conceal
nothing to modify compulsively
a human face that happened to be mine
being nothing more than a set of features in glass
arranged uniquely from others
but otherwise unremarkable.
Dreamed for years
that one day I would be a stoic badass
whose only emotions were punk songs
and the awareness that I had two feet on the ground.
Never crying, never screaming
infinitely mysterious
in every way
my heart tucked back into my collar
away from the hem of my sleeve
more questions than answers
eyes flashing with determination
settling into an everything-proof exoskeleton.
Tonight I careened into my house sobbing
every single shred of good and healthy and sane
confiscated
broken
dirt
as I crashed elbows first
it came back over
this very plot
because this is that one fucking tape loop
gets tucked behind my ear and can't be pried out

I'm so afraid I'm never going to get better
never going to learn that sharp jaw lines and
utilitarian ethics isn't the only look of strength.
I had really hoped
that my rise and fall
wouldn't happen so often.

(untitled)

I know it's a blessed day when I don't look
in the mirror and don't see my birth name
branded on my forehead.
My guardian angel comes in what I can conceal.
The part of me that still aches to conform
To—stick to one box in particular
shares stale air and congealed blood
with the real me—a circus marvel—and it hurts
Behold, lady, gentleman, and other patrons
behold the two headed boy
who's aim in life is to not recognize himself
Nothing in the world has prepared you for a body
that doesn't read the user agreement
or humankind's Terms and Conditions.
Yes, I know
as you study me and try to make me fit in
your mind
you are just as unsettled as I am.
But do not fear
this bone from rib to pelvis to femur
these organs
this aching muscle
is not completely unlike yours
I promise I can be a part of your world
No, you've never had lessons in bodies like mine before
from anywhere
but let me teach you how to look beyond
the spectacle
and touch me.

Um, I'm pretty sure this is gonna be too messy for you
cos, like, I know as you watch me
your mind's eye flips from F to M to probably F again
and maybe M another time
There's only two boxes on your form
And, uh, you've never seen a body like this

I know you haven't
TV never taught you about bodies like mine
and you have to really dig for books on the matter
The truth is—the absolute God's truth is—
I work really hard to feel like my skin fits
And, you know, for a while it didn't, of course
I've not had one of those grounded easy up easy down
swings with my shape where you sorta go haywire from 14 to 18
and then everything's cool and you have your body back.
By that estimation, I'm still in pubescence—
nothing makes sense still—
this is an alien body
but to get my skin to fit
    — takes a teaspoon of hair products
    — one layer of light compression with sport wicking material
    — and another layer that's a vest of shrunken elastic around
      my chest
    — T-shirts and sweaters that aren't too tight or a dead giveaway
      and, trust me, it takes a while to find those
    — jeans that fall in the right spot tightened with a belt
      containing no pink or glitter
    — outerwear that isn't made to hug curves
    — a generous smudge of eyebrow pencil and eye shadow for
      just the right facial contour
    — and a straight spine

All of this, and I too can feel normal.

Pants

I may not know the secrets of the streets
but I know evil in my head
and a heart in flames
and there's no kind of angst like the angst
about what's in my pants
 my angst is between me and my wrongly
crossed legs and how I blush and spread
and all the other little things I forget are best
left to the girls who do it better
all the little lessons I must unlearn
and all of the little bits of would-be shredded confidence
two layers of compression on my chest
straight shoulders
wide stance
one chance
don't call me pretty, I know I'm pretty
damn pretty
elaborate if you would, add a noun
pretty _____ beautiful_____
hint: not girl, not lady, woman's worse
you will inevitably become more confused
the longer your greedy eyes linger on my body
as if I am a lottery, a slot machine
if my face, chest, and crotch all line up similar
congrats
I win for today, but by the measure of strangers
whose brains require the big phallic lever to measure me
in the first place
but if there is a mismatch, if there is a hesitation
I won't need to go to hell
as it has been suggested
I can just glance at each narrowed eye aimed for me
 licking my toes like hot coals for a sacrifice
happily, luckily, I have a theoretical fighting chance
with your eyes through magic tricks I learned
from those, who like me, must be optical illusions

so I will tell you, the actual content of my pants
is of my own making and my own breaking
because there is something fuckable in there, I swear
and now that I know its power
God, am I grateful
but there is something else too
and though it be crafted from common household
objects and a little asymmetrical
I have made great pains to wear it in a way
that will always make it bigger than yours
I was not born into the wrong body—as if it's that simple
like a comma instead of an exclamation point
or the wrong size shirt
if that's the euphemism we're using
we're all in the wrong body
too tall, too fat, too hairy, too pale, so many toos.
We change our physicality to be free from toos
hair dye, makeup, diets, surgery, tattoos, piercings,
new clothes, the gym
so, no, it wasn't the wrong body,
 my body is a respectable rusty rat rod, chopped up,
welded together, stripped, aged, ground down, glued on
and I'm not done yet.
Under all of these tricks is a perfectly acceptable model
objectively speaking, there is no doubt
but it's not anything that I want you to see anymore
under all of these modifications
is something I can only love
as much as a good cry at the end of a long night
insecurity, and yes, angst
and slowly, as I build myself as I see fit
as the slot machine rolls to a win more and more often
my only prayer is that even I
won't recognize it that way anymore
much less you.

Little Freak

Your thoughts were running your thoughts
were running your thoughts were running
while I got up here
I slipped between people in the dark
and all they saw was a some scrawny boy
dipping and weaving in a crooked way
then
shadows
saluting you from behind two goodwill-issue
combat boots that probably have needed repair
for six months or more.
Maybe I caught your eye during someone else's performance
made you curious
maybe
But, ta daaaaaaah! Milo's been announced.
Hello, I stand in position, I begin. I am here.
But wait, you have trouble hearing my words, don't you?
Don't you? You hear a buzzy drone when I speak because
you're distracted.

      I may not know the secrets of the streets
      but I know evil in my head
      and a heart in flames
      and there's no kind of angst like the angst
      about what's in my pants
      my angst is between me and my wrongly
      crossed legs and how I blush and spread
      and all the other little things I forget are best
      left to the girls who do it better
      all the little lessons I must unlearn
      and all of the little bits that girls must remember
Someone in here is thinking "What the fuck is THAT?"
good sir or madam, that is a good question. Very good.
Ponder that some more while you watch me start to squirm.
square my under-developed shoulders and stare back.
Another fun fact, you still want an explanation
"What the fuck is THAT?"

you will inevitably become more confused
the longer your greedy eyes linger on my body
as if I am a lottery, a slot machine
if my face, chest, and crotch all line up similar
congrats
but that's rare
and I'm sorry every day
that I fail
shaky in my boots now
grinding in my teeth
I offer myself freely
to be slain at the altar.
I am not safe. I know.
I am not safe. I am not secure But so help me
I can't keep my lip zipped anymore.
Ladies, Gentlemen, and especially the in between
you may have noticed a lack of volume
in the center of my chest
and down there where my zipper rests
compared to the pitch of my voice
I have an answer.
Fun fact: I spend entire mornings stressed
with the hope I will be invisible. Nothing of note.
Passable.
How? Two layers of compression on my chest,
straight shoulders, hipster glasses
wide stance,
one chance
Pass: to be treated and accepted as one's
preferred gender expression.
I pray that I will at least register
as a giant frozen question, an alien, a he-she
I pray. I pray.
I prayed. And then I looked up at the mirror.
And I looked down.
And prayed my chest was flat enough
willing my body to warp itself into something right.
Eye contact, eye contact!
You have beautiful eyes and a helluva stare, use it.

She said inches from my face
and then in the back of the room
another one of those compliments I prayed for
and then
again
I was a sin, a mistake, a token, a joke
 I became a crime scene for another bigot
there was no bloodstain, no news clipping
no cigarettes laced in DNA
I have no evidence
nothing but what stands before you is the reason why.
        Impossible anatomy skinny as a rail
        perfect cherub lips deep eyes that both
        project galaxies and steal souls
        I know I'm pretty.
        I'm damn pretty.
        Pretty pretty pretty.
        Confusing, considering how hard I tried
        to be pretty to imprison that paradox waiting
        Fun fact: I never did so well at being a girl.
        I spent every day burying her under blowdries
        and raccoon eye makeup and bright red lipstick
        and purple lipstick, black lace and animal print
        flirtation or ally sheedy breakfast club imitation
        Marlboro or Virginia Slim
        layers and layers to forget who was in the mirror
        and what was further south
        Angst slathered in greasepaint, war paint
        but I try not to worry anymore about that
        Oh yes, there is something fuckable in there
        I swear, and now that I know it's power
        God am I grateful.
        Never worry about the equipment beneath.
        Don't fret about this body anymore.
        You don't live in it, you won't touch it
        unless I invite you to.
        Keep your confusion, your irritation, your discomfort
        Leave the living in this body to me, I've got this.

Pomegranate Baby

Pomegranates
have been the subject of myth for centuries
a fruit for the heart
red, dripping, just the right amount of tang
it is told that Eve possibly brought on God's wrath
and the dull roaring aches of birth
by picking the seeds of one for Adam
I never understood, babygirl, how something that small
could sweep grown adults from their feet
and make them willing to endure
hours of ceaseless pain
until this morning
21 weeks inside your mother, the walls
of your home just as red
you are exactly the size of a pomegranate
and as you shifted beneath my fingers
on her navel last night
you shook my soul and stole my heart
and it's all coming together
names dates numbers
snatches of song, softness of skin
who you, little one, will be to me.
Example—WD, the initials of your nickname
40—expected number of weeks in a full term
W
D
40—yes, babygirl, you came to us
to exfoliate our rusty ways of loving
lubricate the locked joints of arms meant for holding
and to quiet our insistent squeaks of protest
your mother and father sat across from me this morning
insisted that if I wasn't ready to take you on
they wouldn't take offense
but how could I turn away from you
after we held hands through your mother?
To love someone or something you can't see

is dangerous
there absolutely is a chance you will get carried away
a chance you will get hurt
but as I gaze at your little face on my phone screen
I can't help but think
with 19 weeks on the clock
how ready I am
for you to break my heart
open

Keep staring, I might do a trick.

Prescription

The rules fucking changed the way they always do:
Somebody told somebody else
that now mental illness is what we want to see
played out in fiction
Depressed people are romantics,
Anxious people are endearing,
Bipolar people are intense,
Schizophrenic people are wildcards,
OCD people are quirky,
Eating-disordered people are delicate and fragile,
PTSD people have great backstory,
and now we're all someone else's favorite character
and everyone wants to be us
which is odd, since WE don't want to be us.

I'm Not Done

Reasons to stay . . .
well,
here's this one thing:
three unfinished books. I carry them
everywhere
these days
talismans
remainders of what used to be
a fully packed backpack
at all times
ready to run for the hills
a Wilde complete works
a Salinger classic
and the least sane Burroughs ever written
barely read
my lover told me that at the very least
I have to find out the endings
all of them
without cheating
that if I ended up on another plane of reality
it'd kill me all over again
cliffhangers over my head
spoilers snacking on my ankles
I'd never forgive myself
he says
he says
he says
the twenty minutes right after
I've woken up
had coffee
are glorious
I'm not sick
I'm not scared
I am funny dreams and the chapter I read last
I'm barely anything at all
before the weight comes down on my shoulders

oh, right, see this?
I have a scruffy gray shadow
that hugs me like a corset
and makes frivolous attempts
to make the space between me and my lover in bed
enormous
too big to reach out and take a hand, offer a kiss
so that it can make quick work of concealing my face
scrubbing into my eyes like tear gas
I'm exhausted. The reel of beatings, bullyings
harassment assault abuse manipulation is draining
But I owe it to Oscar, William, and JD
to, for once, care about someone else's fate.

✳ NOT TODAY ✳

The Sun Will Find You

Yes, you can find your cave and sleep, but know
that the sun will still find you.
And yes, there is still a sun.
I promise you it hasn't left.
The sun is still there just like you are still here.
you can luxuriate in the cotton sheet nest
for as long as necessary
but the sun will still find you
it's ray has a habit of doing that
climbing into bed with you and
tickling your neck when you thought
it'd never come home.
There is something stunning about
waking up after a long night and still being
here.
so be ready to wake up before the sun
brew your coffee, stretch
be awake
be home
be here and be here in defiance
the day was not meant to be fought for
but don't forget that it was also meant to be won.
Smile, because it's not over
and even if you think that midnight is a permanent state,
you will be coated in foggy orange daylight . . .
because that is the way the world works
so be ready to catch the light
eat the apples and the oats and the milk with gratitude.
for the land stretching out around you
telling you it needed water
and air, do not let your fear betray you
and say that your fields and hills are not good.
Your thighs crush empires in any shape!
Your hands make poetry of everything they wrap around!
Your eyes sparkle with cobalt and periwinkle!
Your stomach is your intuition and your nourishment!

Be awake, be home, be here . . .
and be here in defiance
because even if you don't believe
in the daytime at 11:53 p.m.,
at 6:53 a.m. you will tell a different story
the sun will climb into bed with you
and tickle your neck when
you thought it would never come home
because you're awake, you're home, you're here
do not be afraid.

Acknowledgments

The process of putting this book together has been an integral piece in this first year of grieving the loss of my darling child, Allegra/Milo. I'm grateful to those who have accompanied me on this leg of the journey. First, thank you, Grant, my life partner and Milo's dad. You trusted me to honor our child's work and wishes. You have been supportive at every stage of this project. Next, thank you, David, for your love and support of Milo. I have appreciated your advocacy for what you knew Milo would want. Then there's the trio I have called my readers—Candide Jones, Lynn Byrd, and Diana Greene. Along with David, they helped me read through stacks of poetry with objectivity, which I lacked, and the love of words and respect for Milo's life, which we shared. Over the process they did so much more than read poetry. In fact, whenever I reached out for guidance or assistance, they let me tap into their considerable experience and knowledge. They also led me to Press 53 and Kevin Morgan Watson. I am grateful to his willingness to embrace this project and give it a home. I also have to give a shout out to all of the teachers (including, but not limited to, Cherry Kiser, Rodney Coleman, Elroy Windsor, and Jo Dulan,) who encouraged them to write and were intrigued and delighted by Milo's way with words. And to all of their friends who critiqued and collaborated (again including, but not limited to, Jake, Sage, and the Writing Club), Milo found the confidence to share their voice because of you. Finally, I need to express my gratitude for Allegra/Milo for leaving us with such a wealth of work. Thank you for writing things down. Thank you for trusting me enough to share it with me. Thank you for forcing me to be brave and consider aspects of our world that I very well may have missed.

Milo Wright was a poet, a story teller, and a true original, who struggled with physical disabilities, learning disabilities, social awkwardness, gender fluidity, and a willingness to trust that often backfired. Words were their most loyal friend. Milo, born Allegra, began reading before entering school and writing poetry and stories as soon as they figured out how to form the letters. Their poetry is filled with descriptions of these struggles as well as their amazing ability to forgive, to love people for who they were, to try again, and to hang on to hope. Milo, then going by Charlotte, graduated from Middle College at Forsyth Technical Community College in Winston-Salem, North Carolina. On this campus they found safety, a few friends, and their first writing group. This group helped Milo hone their skills and learn to speak to their audience. Another place where Milo found refuge was Trade Street in Winston-Salem, home to The Arts District that often played the role of muse. Whatever their current name of choice—Milo, Charlotte, Ravi, or Allegra— or whatever stage they were passing through, there was someone or someplace on Trade Street to share a conversation or their latest writing or to simply find inspiration for the next poem or play. During their last year, Milo had begun to assemble their writing with the hope of publication. Their life was cut short by an undetected heart defect. After their death, Milo's mother knew the book had to be completed. She searched computers, notebooks, and files for poems and drawings, adding those to what she had rescued over the years from Milo's trash. The result is this intimate compilation of poetry which spans Allegra/Milo's life.

CPSIA information can be obtained
at www.ICGtesting.com
Printed in the USA
BVOW08s1645050417
480346BV00004B/4/P